A HISTORY OF ENGLISH LANGUAGE TESTING IN JAPAN

Masamichi Tanaka

Professor Emeritus, Hiroshima University
Professor Emeritus, Hyogo University of Teacher Education

A HISTORY OF ENGLISH LANGUAGE TESTING IN JAPAN

MASAMICHI TANAKA

KEISUISHA

Hiroshima, Japan

First Published on 15th November, 2008

Copyright ©2008 Masamichi Tanaka

All rights reserved. Not part of this book may be reproduced, stored in a retrieval system, or transmitted in any form or by any means, electronic, mechanical, photocopying, recording, or otherwise, without the prior permission of Keisuisha Publishing Company.

Published by
Keisuisha Co.,Ltd. 1-4, Komachi, Naka-ku, Hiroshima 730-0041
Japan

ISBN978-4-86327-036-7 C3082

ACKNOWLEDGEMENTS

I wish to thank Mr. Albert John Chick, my former colleague of Hyogo University of Teacher Education, and Professor Joe Lauer of Hiroshima University for reading and checking the English from a native speaker's viewpoint. I am further indebted to Professor Tatsunori Takenaka of Kagawa University for his kind help. I am also grateful to many postgraduate students who have attended my course on language testing. Discussions and their comments in the classroom have been a constant source of stimulation.

CONTENTS

ACKNOWLEDGEMENTS ································· *i*
INTRODUCTION ······································ 3

CHAPTER I Development of Educational Evaluation and Assessment of English Language Proficiency ································ 7

CHAPTER II Changes in the Concept of Proficiency in English ································ *23*

CHAPTER III Varieties of Test Types ··············· *61*

CHAPTER IV Entrance Examinations and Students' Abilities in English ···················· *83*

CHAPTER V Evaluation of Communicative Competence ························· *101*

REFERENCES ······································ *121*
INDEX ·· *129*

A HISTORY OF ENGLISH LANGUAGE TESTING
IN JAPAN

INTRODUCTION

Gakusei (The Education System Order), which envisioned the first comprehensive plan for a modern educational system in Japan, was proclaimed by the new Meiji government in 1872, and it was under this Order that English Language Teaching (ELT) was formally and officially established. Although it is, of course, possible to find instances of ELT being practiced before the proclamation of the Order, such efforts were mostly sporadic and local, and were not usually available to the general public.

More than a century has now elapsed since the introduction of the new ELT in the Meiji era, during which time a substantial amount of experience has been acquired in the field. Literature on the general history of ELT is now fairly abundant, and for the most part is readily accessible to those involved in the ELT profession. The same can not be said, however, with regard to the history of language testing. Reviews in the area of language testing have been extremely partial and unsystematic, which, in the author's view, can be ascribed to three rather questionable reasons.

First, since most classroom time has been devoted to instruction related to grammatical structures and vocabulary deemed essential to elementary-level learners, very little room has been available for testing in the entire practice of ELT.

The second reason is the paucity of records in the area of language testing. Normally, quizzes and examination papers actually used in the classroom have been disposed of in the name of confidence immediately after use. The consequent lack of historical records of test items has made systematic investigation extremely difficult.

The third reason is the inclination or furtive willingness of teachers to consign matters related to language testing to a "sanctuary," in which open and frank discussions on quizzes and examinations have been, and to a large extent still are, strictly forbidden. Even today, few teachers are willing to scrutinize or comment on the quality of test items designed by their colleagues, preferring instead to let these "untouchable" remain undiscussed.

With the advent of a new era of Communicative Language Teaching, I believe we have now reached a point where we can no longer afford to avoid discussion of language testing. This is a prerequisite for the production of effective communicative tests for future classroom use.

This book is designed to provide an extensive survey of the development of language testing in Japanese secondary schools and to attempt to foresee the direction classroom testing will take in the future.

CHAPTER I

Development of Educational Evaluation and Assessment of English Language Proficiency

This chapter briefly reviews the development of educational evaluation in the United States and traces its influence on language testing research and practice in Japan.

1.1 Establishment of Educational Evaluation as a Discipline

In this section, a brief survey is made of the development of educational evaluation in the United States. This survey is essential to our review of the growth and advancement of language testing in Japan, since modern, scientific educational evaluation as it is now conceived did not originate in this country, but was transplanted here from the United States.

Shikata (1971, pp.12-14) notes that around the turn of the twentieth century, the measurement movement in the United States suddenly received a boost. This was entirely due to the rapid growth of statistics around that time. The practice of measurement found its way into almost every corner of American society. In the course of time, such new types of tests as intelligence tests, objective tests, and standardized tests appeared one after another, while the key concepts of statistics such as reliability, validity and correlation were adopted rather swiftly by the teaching profession.

The measurement movement culminated in the 1930s. Enthusiasm for the movement cooled because American educators and teachers began to doubt the significance of a practice which had taken on the color of measurement for the sake of measurement. Advocators of the movement rarely reflected on the meaning of measurement, which had come to be implemented mechanically and indiscriminately. Many educators rejected the simple and naïve view that what was measurable could alone be an indicator of human ability. They insisted that other factors or traits which seemed incapable of mechanical measurement should also be considered as essential.

This change of attitude toward the measurement movement was brought about by two new-born theories which also appeared around the 1930s. One was the educational theory proposed by John Dewey (1859-1952), the best known American educator of all time. He rejected the traditional intellectually based and/or logic-centered teaching which was prevalent at the time. He especially opposed dogmatic and authoritarian teaching and rote learning. His motto was "education for man as an entire being." He believed that teaching must foster a cooperative attitude, interest, creativity, and the habit of free inquiry in students, and that these traits were far more essential than the fragmentary knowledge they accumulate during schooling. He insisted that emphasis in teaching should be laid on developing these traits rather than on simply increasing the amount of knowledge. This meant that traits which did not lend themselves to mechanical measurement also needed to be considered as major objectives in the new education. Teachers thus became responsible for weighing the relative values of these traits themselves, and were also obliged to determine the extent to which they should be instilled in their students. Dewey's view on teaching, therefore, reduced the relative value of knowledge-oriented schooling which had characterized the earlier part of the twentieth century.

The other new theory was Gestalt psychology, which originated in Germany around the turn of the century and later found popularity in the United States. The psychology was original and revolutionary to many educators and psychologists at that time. Its basic idea was that human potential could not be divided into separate units, and that wholeness was itself an entity of the human being. "The wholeness is more than the sum of its parts" was a common tenet among Gestalt psychologists. The new psychology soon permeated into American schools, and the very nature of the psychology reduced the value of the data obtained by the then popular techniques which were in essence part-and/or unit-based.

Dewey's new educational theory and Gestalt psychology thus changed the nature of traditional measurement and created an entirely new concept of measurement. This shift of view was represented by the intentional use of the term "evaluation" in place of the then familiar term "measurement" (Hashimoto et al., 1979, pp.19-21).

Unfortunately, this new concept of evaluation conceived in the United States did not reach Japan at that time due to the outbreak of World War II.

1.2 Development of Measurement and Evaluation in ELT in Japan

This section reviews the development of measurement and evaluation in ELT in the Japanese educational setting.

In 1911, Okakura (1868-1936) published a professional book called *Eigo Kyoiku* (Teaching English). This was the first notable work in the early period of ELT in Japan. The book was literally a good guide for in-service teachers at the time, as it touched on issues or items of primary concern among them. Through this work, we can obtain a precise and comprehensive picture of ELT in the Meiji era (1868-1912). A close scrutiny of the book reveals, however, that monumental though the work is, no mention is made of either measurement or evaluation. This indicates that most teachers of English were predominantly absorbed in the methods and techniques available, while their awareness of measurement and evaluation was generally low. The book actually centers mostly on such common topics as effective techniques to use in the classroom, the age when students should start learning English, the aims and values of teaching English, and ways to develop the four skills and to teach grammar.

In the Taisho era (1912-1925), Kaneko's *Kotoba no Kenkyu to Kotoba no Shido* (The Study of Languages and Teaching) appeared in 1923. As the title indicates, the first half of this voluminous work (457 Pp.) is entirely of a general linguistic orientation, while the second half focuses on mother tongue and foreign language teaching in primary and secondary schools. As in Okakura's work, suggestions and recommendations for raising teachers' expertise are given in a general manner. In the final part of his book, Kaneko touches slightly on the question of "marking," to which he devotes four pages. Cautions against subjective marking and the proper allotment of marks are the main topics discussed. The focus of the second half, however, is not on measurement and evaluation, but on language teaching topics in general.

Meanwhile, Harold Edward Palmer (1877-1949) was invited to Japan by the Ministry of Education in 1922. His visit accelerated the modernization of measurement and evaluation miraculously. In his pamphlet entitled *The New-Type Examinations*, he introduced into Japan objective tests that had been developed and used extensively in the United States (Palmer, 1927, pp.1-29). Through this teachers of English in secondary schools were able to familiarize themselves with such new types of "objective" tests, viz. "The True-False Type," "The Selection, or Recognition Type," and "The Completion Type." Unluckily, World War II again intervened, preventing the spread of these objective tests as well as further investigation into the possibilities of their classroom use by teachers.

In the early Showa era (1926-1944), a booklet (49 Pp.) with more discussion directed toward testing was published by Nagahara (1939). His pioneering *Shiken to Gakushu* (Examinations and Learning) covers testing techniques for language classroom in 31 pages. Chapter III is especially rich in content, and the suggestions and advice given were particularly useful and of great help to teachers in setting test items for secondary school students. As a secondary school teacher himself, he strongly recommended that the objective tests which H. E. Palmer introduced be brought into the classroom as a matter of urgency. He included the specimen items of the New-Type Examination in the chapter, hoping that teachers of English would recognize the values and merits of the new-type tests and improve the quality of testing in their classrooms.

Concurrently with the publication of Nagahara's booklet, *Chutogakko Eigokyouzai no Kagakuteki Hensanho* (A Scientific Approach to the Compilation of ELT Materials for Secondary Schools) by Takehara appeared. As the title shows, the focus of the book is not on testing and evaluation, but on materials development. Toward the end of the book, however, Takehara includes a brief section on testing (pp.49-51), showing typical test types commonly used in those days and classifying them into two main categories: standard tests and informal tests. He urged Japanese secondary school teachers to make extensive use of informal tests in their classrooms, and particularly recommended the following types: silent reading tests, multiple choice tests, and completion tests. He firmly believed that by bringing these informal tests into the classroom, the current testing practices, which had been utterly destroyed by translation-centered testing, could be reformed, and that the harmful influence of testing on teaching and learning would thereby be greatly reduced.

During World War II, Gogaku Kyoiku Kenkyusho (The Institute for Research in Language Teaching) issued *Gaikokugo Kyojyuho* (Methods of Teaching Foreign Languages) (2,500 copies). The focus of the book was, again, not on testing and evaluation, but on the methods and techniques which the Institute thought should be adopted to reform the traditional, old-fashioned teaching. The supplement contains a tiny section on "testing" (pp.199-207), and much smaller one on "research in testing" (pp.254-256) is also found in the appendix. In the former section, the immediate introduction of objective tests into the classroom is advocated, while the latter focuses on a variety of test types. Translation into/from Japanese, which was the sole type of test used in the entrance examinations and classroom testing in those days, is severely criticized on the grounds that it failed to obtain data which reflected students' abilities. Six varieties of objective tests which were originally included in A. S. Hornby's *Specimens of New-Type Tests* (1936) are reprinted (IRLT, 1943, pp.201-205). This clearly indicates that the inflow of the information on the new concept of evaluation that had been growing in the United States had been blocked by the war, and that all the Institute could do was simply to represent what H. E. Palmer had introduced in his work some ten years before.

World War II ended in August, 1945 with Japan's defeat, an event that marked a turning point in the development of educational evaluation in this country. Information on the new concept of educational evaluation flooded into new-born Japanese educational circles, and the gaps in the promotion of research in the areas of testing and evaluation was soon filled by a succession of governmental publications. One of these was *The Suggested Course of Study in English for Lower and Upper Secondary Schools (Tentative Plan)*, published in 1951 by the Ministry of Education. This was a revised edition of the 1947 Course of Study which had been drawn up hastily soon after the war. The 1951 revision was indeed a practical and comprehensive source of references for teachers who wished to adopt newer and better methods of organizing the curriculum and of teaching English. Chapter seven dealt specifically with the evaluation of students' progress in English, introducing such key concepts as validity, reliability, and objectivity, and showing examples of numerous types of objective tests for reference. These new types of tests struck teachers as scientific because of the very nature of their objectivity. In fact, this chapter still seems to be an excellent and valuable guide for present-day in-service teachers. Following the issuing of the 1951 Course of Study, objective tests gradually penetrated into the post-war ELT professions.

In the 1950s and 1960s, this penetration was accelerated by the visits of many secondary school teachers to the United States for training. Their encounters with structural linguistics and objective tests were a revelation, and they frequently became disciples of structural linguistics after returning home. What impressed these teachers most was the way in which sentences were analyzed in the new linguistics. Sentences were classified and grouped into patterns according to their structural features. These patterns and/or components of patterns were selected and presented to learners as units of learning, and intensive drills in the sentence patterns then followed. The simplicity and neatness of objective tests were an ideal match for this structural linguistics-based language teaching. Thus, a rather rigid paradigm in ELT was constructed during the 1950s and 1960s, in which structural linguistics was the rationale for the instructional phase and objective tests for the evaluative phase.

However, this paradigm, which had seemed so rigid and stable, began to collapse in the 1970s. It came to be realized that while pattern drills were certainly effective for the mastery of isolated sentences, they did not necessarily lead to the acquisition of communicative competence. Teachers who were disillusioned with structural linguistics-oriented language teaching turned their attention to yet another new approach. Communicative Language Teaching, which originated in Europe and spread rapidly around the world, reached Japan as well. The work of David Wilkins (1976) particularly appealed to Japanese teachers, many of whom were disillusioned with the imperfect outcomes of their teaching. So called "communicative tests" were also introduced to a limited extent, but on the whole they did not attract Japanese teachers' attention. The main reason is probably they were not readily applicable to Japanese ELT settings owing to large class sizes. Thus, no instant shift took place with regard to testing, and it must be admitted that structural tests still remain as the chief tools for assessing communicative competence.

The revised Course of Study issued in 1989, which declared a firm policy to foster a positive attitude toward communicating in a foreign language among secondary school students, obviously heightened teachers' awareness that serious and urgent efforts needed to be made to design and implement communicative tests. In this regard, the presence of the young "Assistant

Language Teachers" invited under the Japan Exchange and Teaching Program (a scheme launched in 1985 and supported by the Ministry of Education, the Ministry of Home Affairs, and the Ministry of Foreign Affairs, often referred to as the JET Program) is a real help in fostering the design and provision of communicative tests for secondary school classrooms. Specimen items of communicative tests developed for a small scale research project started belatedly in the late 1980s are shown for reference in Tanaka (1987, pp. 209-218) and Aoki et al. (1989, pp. 68-80). A more detailed and extensive discussion of communicative language testing is given in Chapter V.

CHAPTER II

Changes in the Concept of Proficiency in English

The nature of the proficiency in English that Japanese ELT educators have expected learners to acquire has varied over the years according to the needs of the times. This chapter reviews changes in the concept of proficiency in English envisaged for the secondary level education from the Meiji era up to the present in order to deepen our understanding of what has been and is meant by language proficiency.

2.1 Proficiency in English Envisaged in the Meiji Era

The demand for skills in foreign languages was extremely high in the period following the Meiji Restoration as the new government adopted an entirely different policy from that of the previous Tokugawa feudal administration. As is well known, the basis of the government's policy was to modernize Japan by importing advanced Western culture and technology. In such a context, foreign languages enjoyed a high standing as the main tool for the acquisition of new knowledge from Western countries. In this regard, the status of English was particularly high in school education in the Meiji era.

2.1.1 English Proficiency Specified in the Middle School Order

The *Chugakkorei* (Middle School Order) [*Chokurei* (Imperial Order) No. 15], promulgated in 1886, was a great step toward the development of secondary education in Japan. Before this, middle schools were regulated by the *Kyoikurei* (Education Order) which came into force in 1879 for the regulation of primary schools. Supervision, which had been incomplete under the Education Order, was tremendously improved by the new Order. Subjects and Their Standards for Ordinary Middle Schools (Ministry of Education Regulations, No.14) appeared in the same year, based on the Middle School Order. Article 5 of the Regulations specified the following eight attainment targets for the first foreign language. (Omura et al., 1980, p. 51):

> Reading aloud
> Reading accompanied by explanation of the text through translation
> Reading followed by instructor's lecture and comments on the content of the text
> Dictation
> Conversation
> Grammar
> Composition

Translation

These targets, however, were too high for secondary school students to attain considering the length of schooling required for graduation (five years).

2.1.2 English Proficiency Prescribed in the 1901 Regulations for the Enforcement of the Middle School Order

The Regulations for the Enforcement of the 1899 Middle School Order (Ministry of Education Regulations, No.3) were issued in 1901. Chapter 1 of the Regulations dealt with Subjects and their Standards, and Article 4 of this chapter defined the objectives and attainment targets as follows (Omura et al., 1980, pp. 70-71).

> Objectives: To develop students' ability to understand normal English, German, or French, and to express themselves in one of

these languages, in order to increase their knowledge.

Attainment Targets:

Pronunciation

Spelling

Reading aloud (*)

Reading accompanied by explanation of the text through translation (*)

Dictation (*)

Composition (*)

Grammar

Conversation

Penmanship

(*) At the outset, simplified texts were to be used. Authentic texts would be introduced in later stages.

It should be noted that in comparison with the attainment targets in the 1886 Order, the contents of the new Regulations were enriched, while the objectives of foreign language teaching were clearly stated. It must also be noted that understanding and the ability to express oneself in English became the main objectives of secondary school ELT. "Reading followed by instructor's lecture and comments on the content of the text" and "Translation" in the previous Regulations were replaced by Pronunciation, Spelling, and Penmanship in the new ones.

2.1.3 English Proficiency Prescribed in the Revised Syllabuses for Middle Schools

The Regulations (1901) mentioned above were revised in 1911. The new syllabuses for middle schools (Ministry of Education Instructions, No.15), based on the revised Regulations (Ministry of Education Regulations, No.26), were issued at the same time. In the new syllabuses, the following attainment targets were included (Omura et al.,1980, p.86).

> Pronunciation
>
> Spelling
>
> Reading aloud and reading accompanied by explanation of the text through translation
>
> Speaking and Composition
>
> Dictation
>
> Penmanship
>
> Grammar

The notable changes were that Speaking replaced Conversation and that two separate attainment targets were integrated into one as Speaking and Composition.

2.2 Proficiency in English Envisaged in the Taisho Era

In the Taisho era, no large-scale statutory revisions were made concerning the subjects and their attainment targets for ordinary middle schools, except that the Ministry of Education reinforced moral education in the revised 1919 Middle School Order (Imperial Order, No.11).

Noteworthy was the rapid expansion of English language teaching in higher elementary schools (Koto Shogakko). Foreign language teaching in higher elementary schools dates back to the Education System Order in the Meiji era. Higher elementary school was not yet compulsory in the Taisho era. However, continued interest in education led to increasing enrollments in these schools. The number of the higher elementary schools in which English was taught was 279 in 1917, this had jumped up to 1,203 by 1926 (Kyokasho Kenkyu Sentaa [Center for Research on School Textbooks], 1984, p.345). The objectives and attainment targets for these students (years seven and eight) were specified in the revised Regulations for the Enforcement of the Elementary School Order (Ministry of Education Regulations, No.6) issued in 1919. Article 16 of the Regulations specified the following objectives of and the attainment targets for foreign language teaching (Okuda, 1985, p.178).

> Objectives and Attainment Targets:
> Pupils should master plain, everyday English. Pupils should be taught pronunciation and spelling first, and then to read simple texts, to speak, and to write. English should be taught by linking the language with pupils' everyday lives in order to promote their understanding and to facilitate drills.

A noticeable characteristic of the above Regulations is that the objectives are exceedingly similar in essence to those in the post-war Course of Study for Lower Secondary Schools.

2.3 Proficiency in English Envisaged in the Early Showa Era

In our review of the concepts of proficiency in English, from this point we will include data from a variety of sources in addition to regulations issued by the central government. By doing so, a more detailed and clearer nature of proficiency will emerge.

2.3.1 Harold E. Palmer's Model of English Proficiency

Harold E. Palmer's view on the ability to use English (or proficiency in English) was extremely comprehensive. He enumerates the following as constituents of proficiency (Palmer, 1927, pp.11-12).

The ability to
(1) recognize isolated English sounds,
(2) pronounce isolated English sounds,
(3) recognize the meaning of certain English intonations,
(4) intone isolated English words,
(5) recognize the spelling of English isolated words when spoken,

(6) recognize the meaning of English isolated words when spoken,

(7) pronounce isolated English words by imitation of a model,

(8) pronounce isolated English words written in phonetic notation,

(9) pronounce isolated English words written in their orthographic form,

(10) spell English words,

(11) understand the meaning or potential meanings of isolated English words when written,

(12) write neatly, legibly or artistically,

(13) write isolated English words in phonetic transcription,

(14) write English connected speech in phonetic transcription,

(15) mark the intonation of an English passage,

(16) read aloud a passage in phonetic transcription,

(17) read aloud a passage in conventional orthography,

(18) understand English prose,

(19) translate English prose into Japanese,

(20) understand conversational English when spoken,

(21) use conversational English,

(22) understand English when spoken or read aloud,

(23) compose English prose,

(24) translate from Japanese into English,

(25) understand the theory of Phonetics,

(26) understand the theory of Intonation,

(27) understand the theory of English Grammar.

Palmer's view of English proficiency is characterized by the fact that aural-oral components amount to one-third of the total proficiency constituents. Palmer's faith in his oral method is thus clearly reflected in his proficiency model.

2.3.2 English Proficiency Specified in the Revised 1931 Syllabuses for Middle Schools

In 1931, the Ministry of Education revised the Regulations for the Enforcement of the Middle School Order in order to introduce innovations into middle level education (Ministry of Education Regulations, No.2). This was the fourth revision of the original Regulations issued in1901. A revision of the syllabuses was also made in accordance with the overall revision (Ministry of Education Instructions, No.5). In the case of foreign languages, however, no fundamental changes were made, so there was little difference between the new syllabuses and those revised in 1911. The new standards specified the following attainment targets (Omura, 1980, p. 126).

    Pronunciation
    Spelling
    Listening

Reading and Interpretation
Speaking and Composition
Dictation
Grammar
Penmanship

2.3.3 Objectives of the American and Canadian Committees on Modern Languages

Around the late 19th and the early 20th centuries, an effort was being made to set goals or objectives which were reasonable and acceptable both to specialists in school education and foreign language teachers, as well as to average secondary school students. Around that time, Japanese middle schools also had to design new syllabuses of their own, based on the guidelines of the revised 1931 Syllabuses for the Middle Schools. Under such circumstances, Nagahara, then a teacher of English in the Middle School affiliated to the Hiroshima

Higher Normal School, considered it significant to inform Japanese secondary school teachers of the objectives proposed by the American and Canadian Committees on Modern Languages. He cited in his article the objectives shown in Algernon Coleman's work (Nagahara, 1932, pp.155-156).

Objectives of the two-year course:
(1) to enable students to read texts which are interesting to them and within the scope of their knowledge and understanding;
(2) to increase students' grammatical knowledge for reading;
(3) to develop accurate pronunciation and aural-oral skills sufficient to be able to understand classroom-level English materials;
(4) to arouse students' interest in foreign countries, their history, and the manners and customs of their people;
(5) to deepen cross-linguistic understanding

of word origins, the meanings of word, and grammar between the students' mother tongue and foreign languages.

Objectives of the three/four-year course:
(1) to develop students' ability to read and widen the scope of their reading, bringing the two abilities closer to those in their native language;
(2) to increase students' grammatical knowledge sufficient for speaking and writing;
(3) to develop students' ability to understand spoken languages;
(4) to increase students' vocabulary and useful expressions for expressing themselves in a foreign language;
(5) to increase students' knowledge of the cultural heritages of foreign countries;
(6) to further students' knowledge of the history of the target language, and deepen cross-linguistic understanding of word origins,

meanings, and grammar between the mother tongue and foreign languages.

The salient features of the above objectives are the emphasis on the development of reading ability and on heightening students' awareness of their mother tongue.

2.3.4 English Proficiency Envisaged in the Syllabus Drawn up by the English Department of the Middle School Affiliated to Hiroshima Higher Normal School

In accordance with the revision of the Syllabuses for Middle Schools (1931) mentioned above, Takahashi (1931, pp.12-13) of the English Department of the Middle School affiliated to Hiroshima Higher Normal School proposed a new ELT syllabus for the school. The syllabus listed the following attainment targets, each of which was to be apportioned across five years of schooling.

> Year 7 (12 year-olds)
>> Pronunciation
>> Spelling
>> Word form
>> Usage
>> Listening to simple words, phrases and passages
>> Reading and interpretation
>> Dictation
>> Speaking and writing in simple English
>> Penmanship
>
> Year 8 (13 year-olds)
>> Attainment targets for Year 7 are applied.
>> Furthering listening, reading and dictation skills
>
> Year 9 (14 year-olds)
>> Attainment targets for Year 8 are applied.
>> Outline of grammar
>
> First course (3 hrs/week)
>
> Year 10 (15 year-olds)
>> Attainment targets for Year 9 are applied.

Furthering listening, reading and dictation skills
　Furthering speaking and writing skills
Year 11 (16 year-olds)
　Attainment targets for Year 10 are applied.
Second course (5-6 hrs/week)
Year 10
　Attainment targets for Year 9 are applied.
　Furthering listening, reading and dictation skills
　Furthering speaking and writing skills
　Outline of grammar
Year 11
　Listening to words and phrases, or passages in ordinary English
　Furthering speaking and writing skills

2.4 Proficiency in English Envisaged in the Late Showa Era

After World War II, large scale educational reform was enforced by the occupation authorities. In carrying out this reform, the Report of the United

States Education Mission to Japan (1946) was essential and became the official guideline. The Mission was sent by the U. S. government at the request of the General Headquarters, which had been established to oversee the Japanese government in 1945. The Report was indeed a comprehensive plan for restructuring the entire Japanese educational system.

The old militaristic educational system was soon abolished, and the new postwar system of education started with the promulgation of the School Education Law in 1947.

The former Syllabuses for Middle Schools and the Subjects and Their Standards for Ordinary Middle Schools no longer remained in effect. Proficiency in English was hereafter specified by Courses of Study which were introduced to regulate the new-born secondary education comprehensively.

2.4.1 Ability to Use English Specified in the 1947 Course of Study for English (Tentative Plan)

One year after the publication of the Report of the U. S. Education Mission to Japan, the Outline of the 1947 Courses of Study (Tentative Plan) was published for elementary and lower and higher secondary schools and the respective Course of Study for each subject hurriedly followed (Ministry of Education, 1980, pp. 241-242). The Course of Study for English was a small 28-page booklet with 5-page appendix on pronunciation at the back.

Four overall objectives for lower and higher secondary school were listed (Research Group on Postwar Educational Reform Materials, National Institute for Educational Research, 1980, pp.1-2):

(1) to enable students to think in English;
(2) to enable students to understand English and speak in English;

(3) to enable students to read and write in English;

(4) to introduce students to English-speaking peoples, particularly their manners, customs, and daily lives.

The above four objectives in the Tentative Plan are, to the eye of a present-day teacher, the very prototype of the language abilities that has survived in the later Courses of Study revised since then several times. The first objective was obviously too demanding, considering the devastating and chaotic educational circumstances and the extremely limited number of trained teachers just after the War. The other three objectives closely resemble those in the current Course of Study for junior and senior high schools.

2.4.2 Ability to Use English Specified in the 1951 Revised Course of Study for English (Tentative Plan)

The 1947 Course of Study for English introduced hastily to the postwar ELT profession was replaced by a new Course of Study in 1951. Compared with the preceding one, this Course was richer in content in every respect. Research findings and innovative ideas from the period during and immediately after the War were fully incorporated in the voluminous new Course (759 pp.). Also, all the chapters were written in English as well as in Japanese. The Preface explains that "the decision to write the volume in English was made so that it might be of value in seminars and to foreign teachers who cannot read Japanese." (Research Group, 1980, ii).

Three broad aims were established for ELT in Lower Secondary Schools (Research Group, 1980, pp. 14-16):

A. Overall Aim

To develop a practical basic knowledge of English as "speech" with primary emphasis on aural-oral skills and the learning of structural patterns through learning experiences conducive to mastery in hearing, oral expression, reading, and writing, and to develop as an integral part of the same an understanding of, appreciation for, and a desirable attitude toward the English-speaking peoples, especially as regards their modes of life, manners, and customs.

B. Major Functional Aims

(1) To develop skills in listening, with understanding, to English as "speech," the standard being that generally accepted as suitable for stages of development of pupils of the lower secondary school, so that

(a) in developing skills in aural-oral experiences the skills acquired in listening (1) may prove of practical value within the standard of the lower secondary school and (2) may serve as a sound foundation for those taking more advanced work in or outside the upper secondary school,

(b) in developing skills in reading or writing experiences the skills acquired in listening may serve as a necessary foundation and criterion for the acquisition of such skills.

(2) To develop skills in oral expression in English as "speech," of a standard generally accepted as being suitable for the lower secondary school, so that

(a) in the case of those students who may wish to acquire skills in oral expression in particular, the skills acquired (1) may prove of practical value within the standard generally accepted as suitable for stages of development of pupils of the lower secondary school and (2) may serve as a sound foundation for those taking more advanced work in or outside of the upper secondary school,

(b) in developing skills in reading or writing experiences the skills acquired in oral expression may serve as a necessary foundation and criterion for the acquisition of such skills.

(3) To develop skills in reading English as "speech" with understanding, of a standard generally accepted as being suitable for stages of development of pupils of the lower secondary school, so that

(a) in developing skills in writing experiences the skills acquired in reading (1) may prove of practical value within the standard of the lower secondary school and (2) may serve as a sound foundation for those taking more advanced work in or outside the upper secondary school,

(b) in developing skills in writing experiences the skills acquired in reading may serve as a necessary criterion and complement in the acquisition of such skills.

(4) To develop skills in writing English as "speech" of a standard generally accepted as being suitable for stages of development of pupils of the lower secondary school, so that

(a) the skills (1) may prove of practical value within the standard of the lower secondary school and (2) may serve as a sound foundation for those taking more advanced work in or outside of the upper secondary school.

C. Major Cultural Aims

(1) To develop an understanding of, appreciation for, and a desirable attitude toward the modes of life, manners, and customs of English-speaking peoples, as an integral

part of the English course, so that

(a) in developing skills in listening, oral expression, reading, and writing, the learning experiences may not be divorced from the modes of life, manners, and customs of English-speaking people whose language is an integral part of their cultures,

(b) the development of such an appreciation and attitude may serve as a sound foundation for those taking more advanced work in or outside of the upper secondary school,

(c) the development of such an appreciation and attitude, together with the linguistic skills acquired, may contribute toward students' individual, social, vocational competence,

(d) the development of such an appreciation and attitude, together with the linguistic skills acquired, may serve as an important part in education for peace.

It can safely be said that the overall aim and the other two broad aims established by the revised Course of Study were basically identical in nature to those set out in the 1947 Course. Terms such as "skills" and "English as speech," however, were strikingly innovative and appealing to many administrators and teachers at that time.

2.4.3 "Structure" of Abilities in English

A totally new approach to defining proficiency in English appeared in the early 1960s. Formerly, proficiency had been defined solely by listing or enumerating the objectives or skills/subskills involved. The new approach was different in that it attempted to assemble the assumed constituents into integrated, structured constructs and to show their internal "structure."

Thus, the structures of reading and writing

abilities were formulated as follows (Hatori, 1962, pp.94-98):

> Ability in reading
> = capacity to grasp the content × speed
> Ability in writing
> = capacity to construct grammatical sentence(s)
> × knowledge of vocabulary

Contrary to the ostentatious, seemingly original naming, the proposed structures were surprisingly simple and naïve.

Some thirty years later, the above hypotheses were improved by the same author (Ando et al., 1991, pp. 43-45).

> (1) Ability in writing
> = knowledge of vocabulary [P] × capacity to construct grammatical sentences [P] + α
> P = production
> α = logicality, common sense, literary talent,

etc.

(2) Ability in reading

= knowledge of vocabulary [R] × capacity to construct grammatical sentences [R] + α

R = recognition

(3) Ability in listening

= knowledge of vocabulary [SR] × capacity to construct grammatical sentences [SR] + α

SR = sound recognition

(4) Ability in speaking

= knowledge of vocabulary [SP] × capacity to construct grammatical sentences [SP] + α

SP = sound production

These improved hypotheses were nevertheless the same in nature as those given previously.

2.4.4 Proficiency in English in Structural Linguistic Days

Assuming that objectivity is one of the conditions

for the modernization of language testing, the contribution made by the structural linguistics must be acknowledged. Lado (1961) was particularly influential in the campaign for objectivity in language testing. The new view on proficiency was characterized by its emphasis on the elements of language as the components of proficiency. In concrete terms, it was hypothesized that proficiency is comprised of the skills and elements of language, among which are pronunciation, grammatical structure, vocabulary, and cultural meaning.

In the early 1970s, Tsuchiya (1973, pp. 60-63) proposed the following structural linguistics-oriented model of proficiency.

Listening ability
= ability to apply knowledge and skills concerning the sub-components below in contexts (situations):
(a) phonological knowledge and the skills to discriminate sounds aurally;

(b) knowledge of vocabulary and the skills to discriminate words aurally;

(c) structural knowledge and the skills to discriminate structures aurally.

Speaking ability

= ability to apply knowledge and skills concerning the sub-components below in contexts (situations):

(a) phonological knowledge and the skills to pronounce sounds orally;

(b) knowledge of vocabulary and the skills to produce words orally;

(c) structural knowledge and the skills to produce grammatical structures orally.

Reading ability

= ability to apply knowledge and skills concerning the sub-components below in contexts (situations):

(a) orthographical knowledge and the skills to discriminate spellings visually;

(b) knowledge of vocabulary and the skills to

discriminate words visually;

(c) structural knowledge and the skills to discriminate structures visually.

Writing ability
= ability to apply knowledge and the skills concerning the sub-components below in contexts (situations):

(a) orthographical knowledge and the skills to spell words correctly;

(b) knowledge of vocabulary and the skills to spell words correctly;

(c) structural knowledge and the skills to produce grammatical structures in written forms.

It must be noted that Tsuchiya viewed proficiency as dynamic and performative, as is evident from the fact that he emphasized the language learners' ability to apply the knowledge and the skills they had acquired in actual contexts. The proficiency model based on structural linguistics, it seems, lent itself to ELT in Japanese setting, especially to the beginning and pre-intermediate levels, when learners were obliged to learn language elements one by one in their classrooms. Even today, this model is popular among lower secondary school teachers who teach English as a foreign language.

2.4.5 English Proficiency in Post-structural Days

Needless to say, efforts to develop better models of proficiency continue to be made by the ELT profession. The current endeavor is to break away from the structural linguistics-based model as it is believed not to reflect the pragmatic nature of language adequately. Teachers and learners of today are more concerned with language as "use" rather than as "usage." In other words, their interest does not lie in language described abstractly, but in language as it is used in speakers' everyday lives for communication. This change of attitude toward language and language learning was obviously brought about by the upsurge in sociolinguistics in the 1970s. It was natural that this change should prompt researchers in the EFL/ESL field to construct afresh a new concept of proficiency that is valid and viable in the communicative language teaching milieu.

According to Valdman, Sandra Savignon was the first to propose the sociolinguistics-based concept of proficiency under the name "communicative competence." He cites her definition as follows (Valdman, 1978, p. 567):

> Communicative competence may be defined as the ability to function in a truly communicative setting, that is, in a dynamic exchange in which *linguistic competence* must adapt itself to the total informational output, both linguistic and paralinguistic, of one or more interlocutors.

Eleven years later, her communicative competence

took a more concrete form with the inclusion of four components in the model: grammatical competence, sociolinguistic competence, discourse competence, and strategic competence (Savignon, 1983, pp.45-46). Savignon's original model was introduced into Japanese ELT circles rather swiftly, together with communicative tests designed after the model for classroom use (Tanaka, 1987, pp. 209-218).

Savignon's model was later refined by Bachman (1980, p. 87), who coined the term "language competence" to denote his views on language ability. His language competence comprises two types of competence as macro components: organizational competence and pragmatic competence. Each of these, in turn, consists of two sub-competences respectively: organizational competence is comprised of grammatical competence and textual competence, while pragmatic competence consists of illocutionary competence and sociolinguistic competence. Bachman's model was also promptly introduced into Japanese secondary schools (Aoki et al., 1989, iv). Not a few teachers are now familiar with the model, and new types of tests, called "communicative tests," are being developed and utilized in innovative classrooms.

This chapter has reviewed chronologically the nature of the proficiency in English that Japanese secondary school students have been expected to acquire in their schooling during the past century. Through this review, it has become clear that ideas on what constitutes proficiency have differed from period to period, and that the proficiency models envisaged have become more elaborate and refined as time has gone by.

CHAPTER III

Varieties of Test Types

This chapter reviews the varieties of test types that have been commonly used in secondary school English language teaching since the Meiji era. Through this survey, it is hoped that the process by which classroom tests/quizzes have evolved and diversified will be made clear.

3.1 Varieties of Tests/Quizzes Appearing in Authorized English Textbooks

From the Meiji era to the present, an enormous diversity of English textbooks have been issued. This review of the test types will focus on English grammar textbooks, since they contain a far greater variety of tests than any other textbooks.

(1) Naibu Kanda's *HIGHER ENGLISH GRAMMAR* (Revised Edition) Tokyo: Sanseido, 1904

   Students are required to:

   (a) classify

   ① nouns (material noun, abstract noun, common noun)

   ② verbs (intransitive verb vs. transitive verb; regular verb vs. irregular verb)

   ③ adverbs (place, time, quantity, manner)

   ④ parts of speech (pronoun, adverb, preposition)

   (b) tell/write

   ① meanings of the words in sentences

   ② adjective forms of the noun

   (c) parse

   ① words, phrases, clauses

   ② subjects, predicates,

   ③ main clauses, dependent clauses

(d) correct (grammatical) errors
(e) translate Japanese into English
    ① free translation
    ② guided translation (using interrogative pronouns, particles, to-infinitives, gerunds)
(f) fill in the blanks
    ① relative pronouns
    ② prepositions, prepositional phrases
    ③ connectives
(g) rewrite
    ① active voice → passive voice ; passive voice → active voice
    ② direct objects → indirect objects ; indirect objects → direct objects
    ③ direct narration → indirect narration ; indirect narration → direct narration
(h) substitute
    ① pronouns
    ② relative pronouns
(i) omit the omissible part(s)

As is to be expected, the above items mainly tested students' lexical, morphological, and syntactical knowledge. Test items of types (e) and (f) were specifically favored. The types of tests included are impressively diverse for a textbook published in the Meiji era. This is obviously a reflection of Okakura's expertise and competence as a leading figure in the ELT field.

(2) Kenjiro Kumamoto's *ELEMENTARY GRAMMAR* Tokyo: Kaiseikan, 1918

Students are required to:

(a) classify

① nouns

② parts of speech

③ simple sentences, complex sentences, compound sentences

(b) show knowledge of vocabulary

① antonyms

② plurals of nouns, adjective forms of nouns

③ present participles

④ conjugation of verbs

(c) parse

① subjects, predicates (subjects, verbs)

② complements

③ adjective phrases, adverbial phrases

(d) translate Japanese into English

① partial translation

② full translation

(e) compose sentences using given words and phrases

(f) fill in the blanks

① prepositions

② definite (indefinite) articles

(g) rewrite

① direct objects → indirect objects; indirect objects → direct objects

② active voice → passive voice; passive voice → active voice

③ negative sentences, interrogative sentences, exclamatory sentences

④ comparative degree

⑤ participial construction

⑥ subjunctive mood

⑦ using 'have'

(h) translate English into Japanese

(i) paraphrase

As in Kanda's textbooks, various sorts of test types were included by Kumamoto. A novel feature is the adoption of partial translation from Japanese into English to reduce the learner's burden. Another innovation is the introduction of translation from English into Japanese. Interestingly, test type (d) was particularly favored in this textbook as it was in Kanda's.

(3) Hiroshi Katayama's *FIRST ENGLISH GRAMMAR* Tokyo: Kenkyusha, 1918

Students are required to:

(a) classify

① sentences (declarative, interrogative,

imperative, exclamatory)

　② verbs (intransitive, transitive)

　③ sentence patterns

　④ phrases (noun, adjective, adverbial)

　⑤ conjunctions

　⑥ interrogative / relative pronouns

(b) show knowledge of vocabulary

　① proper nouns

　② singular / plural of nouns

　③ comparative degree

　④ case of pronouns

　⑤ conjugation of verbs

(c) parse

　① subjects, verbs, objects, complements

　② adjectives, adverbs (adverbial phrases)

　③ subordinate clauses

(d) translate Japanese into English

(e) compose sentences using given words and phrases

(f) fill in the blanks

　① nouns, pronouns

② verbs, auxiliary verbs

③ relative pronouns

④ conjunctions

⑤ articles

(g) rewrite

① pronouns (I → She)

② active voice → passive voice ; passive voice → active voice

③ sentence patterns

④ negative sentences, interrogative sentences

(h) substitute (using pronouns)

(i) complete (omitted words and phrases)

(j) recite

The new test type worth noting in Katayama's textbook is recitation.

(4) Kaiseikan's *GIRL'S EASY GRAMMAR* (Revised edition) Tokyo: Kaiseikan, 1937

Students are requested to:

(a) classify

(As the items listed under each task are quite similar to those shown in the preceding three textbooks, details are omitted hereafter.)

(b) show knowledge of vocabulary

(c) parse

(d) correct ungrammatical sentences

(e) translate Japanese into English

(f) fill in the blanks

(g) rewrite

(h) translate English into Japanese

(i) insert / omit words and phrases

It can be seen that most of the above test types are essentially the same as those used in the previous textbooks published in the Meiji and Taisho eras.

(5) Chutogakko Kyokasho Kabushikikaisha's *English I* (Parts 1-3) Tokyo: Chutogakko Kyokasho Kabushikikaisha (Secondary

School Textbook Company), 1946
Students are required to:
(a) show knowledge of vocabulary
(b) translate Japanese into English
(c) fill in the blanks
(d) rewrite
(e) ask and answer in English
(f) select / choose

This three-part textbook series, which was an expurgated publication based on pre-war national textbooks, is noteworthy in that it marked the first appearance of multiple-choice tests.

(6) Ministry of Education's *Let's Learn English* (Books 1-3) Tokyo: Kyoiku Tosho, 1947
Students are required to:
(a) classify
(b) show knowledge of vocabulary
(c) translate Japanese into English
(d) translate English into Japanese

(e) fill in the blanks
(f) compose sentences (partial composition)
(g) ask and answer in English
(h) choose (three alternatives)
(i) match

Objective tests, like multiple-choice test and matching test, which Harold E. Palmer had strongly recommended before the War, are used more extensively than in the preceding textbook.

3.2 Varieties of Tests / Quizzes Used in Students' Study Books

There was not a single middle school student in the Taisho and Early Showa eras who did not know S. Yamazaki (1883-1930) and Keijiro Ono (1869-1952). Students preparing for entrance examinations to Higher and Specialized Schools would have all perused study books authored either Yamazaki or Ono, the two 'gurus' of the crambook world before

World War II. Among middle school students the former was called 'Yama-Tei' and the latter 'Ono-Kei.' Generally, Yamazaki's works were considered more difficult and advanced, while Ono's were thought easier to understand.

Here, Yamazaki's well-known grammar book will be examined.

> *Jishu Eibunten* (English Grammar Self-Taught)
> Tokyo: Kenkyusha, 1913
> Students are required to:
> (a) classify
> (b) show knowledge of vocabulary
> (c) correct errors
> (d) translate Japanese into English
> (e) fill in the blanks
> (f) rewrite
> (g) ask and answer in English
> (h) omit (relative pronouns)

Out of these eight test types, (c), (d), and (f) were

particularly favored.

3.3 Varieties of Tests/ Quizzes Used in Year-End Examinations

In spite of Harold E. Palmer's efforts to bring about the introduction of objective tests (Palmer named them 'New-Type Examinations') into Japanese classrooms on an extensive basis, most teachers were slow to respond to his expectations. In such a milieu, Jiyu Gakuen, a private school founded in Tokyo in 1921 by Motoko Hani and her husband, was one of the earliest to introduce objective tests into its classrooms. The following year-end examination was given to the preparatory class there in 1933. It is based on *Helen Keller*, vol. 8 of the "English as Speech Series" published by the Institute for Research in English Teaching. The series consisted of 12 volumes of popular stories simplified for upper-grade Middle and Higher School intensive reading classes. (One question which is not in the nature of a 'New-Type' test is omitted (Palmer, 1933, pp. 5-6).

1. Here are 10 statements. Some are true and others are not true. If you think the statement is true, put a ring round the letter R; if you think the statement is not true, put a ring round the letter W.

    20 points:

    A right answer gives you 2 points.

    A wrong answer takes away 2 points.

    No answer at all neither gives you points nor takes them away.

R. W. 1. Miss Keller could read and write with her bright eyes when she was ten years old.

R. W. 2. A deaf child cannot hear the speech of other people.

R. W. 3. When Helen could not make people understand her, she became very angry.

Varieties of Test Types 75

R. W. 4. Miss Sullivan came to Helen's house to live as her nurse, but she did not like her.

R. W. 5. Helen read French and German for pleasure before she knew the grammar.

R. W. 6. Helen determined to enter Radcliffe College which belongs to Columbia University.

R. W. 7. Helen is blind, yet she sees and understands more clearly with her mind than many people do with their eyes.

R. W. 8. Helen Keller is sometimes compared with Newton.

R. W. 9. Helen's life has been an inspiration to many people.

R. W. 10. Helen sometimes feels lonely, because she does not trust in God.

— : : —

2. Write between each pair of parentheses an appropriate article (a, an, the, or [ ]). [ ]

indicates no article.

20 points:

A right answer gives you 2 points.

A wrong answer takes away 2 points.

No answer at all neither gives you points nor takes them away.

1. Helen had ( ) serious illness when she was ( ) little child.
2. ( ) blindness sometimes comes as the result of ( ) illness.
3. ( ) man or woman who writes a book is called ( ) author.
4. Is it easier for ( ) deaf person to learn to speak or for ( ) deaf and blind person to learn?
5. Miss Sullivan changed ( ) subject for ( ) little while.
6. Helen sometimes asked ( ) teacher ( ) meaning of some words.
7. Helen went to ( ) sea for ( ) first time when she was nine years old.

8. Helen had always swum in ( ) rivers or ( ) lakes where the water was fresh.
9. ( ) most famous book written in ancient Greek is ( ) Iliad.
10. It is a good thing to read without using ( ) dictionary or ( ) notes.

— ∷ —

3. Write between each pair of parentheses an appropriate preposition.

10 points:

A right answer gives you 1 point.

A wrong answer takes away 1 point.

No answer at all neither gives you points nor takes them away.

1. ( ) her anger she would kick and ( ) her grief she would cry out.
2. ( ) vigorous strokes she sent a stream of water ( ) the cup.
3. Helen liked to ride ( ) someone else ( ) a bicycle with two seats.
4. Miss Sullivan came ( ) the Keller home

and began to teach Helen (　　) March 3, 1887.

5. (　) using a language we can quickly become acquainted (　) its literature.

6. She has learnt to speak (　) feeling (　) her fingers the mouth, face and throat of anyone who is speaking to her.

7. (　) 1880, three years after Miss Sullivan came to the Keller home, Helen could "talk" readily (　) her fingers.

8. It would have been quite impossible (　) Miss Keller to work as she has done (　) a strong body and sound nerves.

9. A student learning a foreign language might take a hint (　) Helen's rapid development (　) such conditions.

10. Helen tells us that in her first examinations (　) Radcliffe College she received "honours" (　) German and English.

—∷—

4. Some of the words below are spelt correctly;

others incorrectly. If you think the word is spelt correctly, put a ring round the letter R; if you think the word is spelt incorrectly, put a ring round the letter W.

20 points:
> A right answer gives you 1 point.
> A wrong answer takes away 1 point.
> No answer at all neither gives you points nor takes them away.

R. W. 1. descrive

R. W. 2. comunicate

R. W. 3. successfully

R. W. 4. phisycal

R. W. 5. punishment

R. W. 6. dramatically

R. W. 7. foundamental

R. W. 8. conception

R. W. 9. pump

R. W. 10. bocavulary

R. W. 11. courageous

R. W. 12. methode

R. W. 13. conscious

[sic.]

R. W. 15. scenery

R. W. 16. grammer

R. W. 17. essential

R. W. 18. liesure

R. W. 19. process

R. W. 20. ensuthiastic

— : : —

5. Supply the necessary word between each pair of parentheses.

   10 points:

     A right answer gives you 1 point.

     A wrong answer takes away 1 point.

     No answer at all neither gives you points nor takes them away.

1. Greek is an ( ) language. It is also called a ( ) language.
2. Radcliff is a ( ) attended by ( ) only.
3. Helen Keller is quite ( ) ; she cannot see ( ) at all.

4. Miss Sullivan (　　) the names of things in Helen's (　).
5. Miss Fuller's (　　) and lips moved when she (　).
6. Helen began to study (　) languages (　) she was young.
7. Helen took (　) from her (　) tutors.
8. Helen had to pass the entrance (　　) in order to (　) Radcliff College.
9. Helen Keller is an (　　) woman who is famous because she has become highly educated in spite of unusual (　).
10. Let us see how she studied to (　　) the (　) languages.

In this chapter, we have reviewed the evolution and diversification of classroom tests / quizzes, particularly of objective tests. Through this review, it has become clear that with the exception of a few pioneering private institutions Harold E. Palmer's endeavors were appreciated rather belatedly.

CHAPTER IV

Entrance Examinations and Students' Abilities in English

It has often been said that entrance examinations to upper schools dominate the entire teaching carried out in lower schools. Lower schools are, therefore, compelled to adjust their teaching to the entrance examinations imposed on them by upper schools, regardless of the quality of such examinations.

In this chapter we shall focus on the controversy over entrance examinations administered in the past and the standards of students who sat for them.

4.1 The Status Quo in Entrance Examinations to Higher and Specialized Schools in the Meiji Era

Around the end of the Meiji era, Ishikawa (1911, pp. 19-28), a professor of Tokyo Higher Normal School which admitted Normal / Middle School graduates, lamenting the then devastating entrance examinations to state schools, made the following recommendations for urgent reform.

(1) We should attempt to match question items with students' ability levels. The question items should also have discriminatory functions. For that purpose, we should mingle a variety of questions, ranging from simple to difficult ones. A fair allotment of marks should also be made in proportion to the relative weight of each item.

(2) We should not use texts taken directly from the middle school textbooks for test

construction.

(3) Marking criteria, together with general guidelines for the standardization of marking, should be stated clearly and shown to teachers.

(4) We should avoid setting items which are appropriate only for the best students and which are advantageous to students who have relevant specific background knowledge. Care should be taken to diversify items so that they are representative and comprehensive.

(5) Texts for reading comprehension tests should be autonomous and coherent. They should also be varied in content and interesting to the students. The old-fashioned proverbial or anecdotal texts, morality stories, and sloppy texts should be avoided.

(6) Japanese sentences for English translation should be easy to understand and clear

in meaning. We often find strange turns of expressions and unclear Japanese sentences.

(7) In grammar tests, the focus of assessment should not be placed solely on the amount of students' grammatical knowledge, but on their ability to use it.

(8) At present, there seem to be no definite guidelines on the teaching of dictation and its evaluation. We should, first and foremost, allot proper marks for dictation in accordance with its relative weight in the entire examination. A marking scheme for teachers' reference based, for instance, on the number of correct / incorrect syllables or letters should be provided to ensure reliable marking. A classification of foreseeable errors should also be made so that teachers can deduct marks consistently.

(9) Personal preferences and biases in question setting should be avoided by introducing a

variety of question items. It is advisable to make use of realia or visuals for composition tests. Listening comprehension tests and summarizing or gist telling of longer texts may also be included.

Ishikawa pressed for the above nine recommendations to be put into practice immediately so that ELT in middle schools could survive. He stressed that reforming the entrance examinations would also exert a beneficial influence on the overall quality of the ELT in higher and specialized schools.

4.2 Criticism of Examinees' Abilities in English on the Higher School Side in the Taisho and Early Showa Eras

In the Taisho era, Kimura, a professor of Yamaguchi Higher Commercial School, analyzed candidates' answers of English entrance examinations given by his school. His minutely detailed analysis is an invaluable record from which we can obtain a clear picture of middle school students' abilities in English at that time. It reveals the existence of a vast gap or discrepancy between the high expectations on the side of Higher School and middle school students' actual abilities in English. Kimura found and classified the following errors (Kimura, 1917, pp. 1-7).

(1) They often confuse the meaning and proper use of common words and phrases.
to know vs. to learn
to reach vs. to arrive
necessity vs. necessary
hard vs. hardly
foolish vs. ignorant
respectful vs. respectable
Empire vs. Emperor
infancy vs. infantry / fancy
pleasure vs. treasure
absolute vs. abstract

(2) They make mistakes in spelling arising from incorrect pronunciation and careless observation.
  (a) Misspelling of such common words as parents, school, library, dictionary
  (b) storong < strong
    handored < hundred
    barious < various
    horegner < foreigner
    Rondon < London
  (c) frome < from
    yeare < year
    appeare < appear
    halfe < half
  (d) strang < strange
    Europ < Europe
    natur < nature
(3) They pay little attention to the construction of English sentences. The result is that their translation is sometimes entirely wrong, or even utterly unintelligible, and

their English often presents the curious spectacle of a language constructed on strict grammatical principles, yet scarely genuine English.

(Examples are not shown.)

(4) They do not know fundamental, elementary grammar.

(a) Mistakes in the use of number and person of verbs:

They does not know

The battle have take place

My parents loves me

When I was children

(b) Confusion in the use of tenses and auxiliary verbs:

I must be seemed

It must be seems

It must be to seem

The custom is must be seemed to be strange.

I have went to the library.

The European was have been begans.

The another of the book had been comes.

(c) Confusion in the use of transitive / intransitive verbs and mixing up parts of speech:

(Examples are not shown.)

(d) Improper use of preposition and article:

I have went library.

I went at library.

When comes time of peace of its

Notwithstanding beyond year has passed

In order to I have preparation

I am not doubt

We unknow

I have been many experience

I have had many experienced

Later, at the beginning of the Showa era, Watari, a professor of Yokohama Specialized School, likewise, examined the papers of some 1,000 applicants to his school. The results reported were similar to those obtained at Yamaguchi Higher

Commercial School (Watari, 1938, pp. 49-51).

(1) Students' knowledge of vocabulary is poor. They make mistakes in spelling such common words as:

foriegner / forigner < foreigner
nipon < Japan
Japanes / japanese < Japanese
therefor < therefore
sometime < sometimes
some what < somewhat
mak / maker < make
then < them
off < of
frome < from
butiful < beautiful
feild < field
Itali < Italy
Germani < Germany
full / fol < fool
folish < foolish

questione < question
deside < decide
meny < many
seldome < seldom
speek < speak
carless < careless
harry < hurry
theyselves < themselves
becose < because
of cause / of corse < of course
presentative < representative
industing / undistanding < understanding

(2) Students' fundamental knowledge of English grammar is poor.

(a) Syntactic errors:

They sometimes that

When we don't such a thing

We hence foreigners that

Foreigners often determination that

(b) Misuse of finite verbs:

Foreigners are agree

Japan was seem

They had mistaken understand

(c) Errors in the number and person of verbs:

The Japanese delegates often was

All country of the world

Some matter happen

Japan have

She have

We are fool

(d) Imperfect knowledge of the passive voice:

We are think

being understand

We are stupid by foreigners.

(e) Imperfect knowledge of adjectives:

It is so much difficulty.

We are foolishness.

Errors similar to those given above are still found in today's secondary school students' daily performance.

4.3 Complaints by Middle Schools about Entrance Examinations to Higher and Specialized Schools in the Early Showa Era

Twenty years after Ishikawa's proposals for reform, Matsuoka, a teacher of Osaka Prefectural Toyonaka Middle School, investigated the questions for entrance examinations to 104 state and private higher and specialized schools. He sorted all the items in the English examinations according to the skills tested (Matsuoka, 1932, pp. 134-147). The results show that only four varieties of skills were tested: translation into Japanese, translation into English, English grammar, and dictation. It is surprising that the great majority of the schools surveyed uniformly included only the first two varieties in their examinations. The number of schools testing English grammar was 14, while in the case of dictation it was even smaller (7 schools). Another finding was that the average numbers of questions set for the first and second skills were 3.41 and 2.12 respectively.

Judging from the above survey, there had actually been no conspicuous reform of entrance examinations to upper schools. Ishikawa's proposals made twenty years earlier had been virtually ignored, and what might be called a "national prototype" of the entrance examinations had become moulded and even cherished as an almost permanent fixture. Matsuoka criticized the arrogant and insensible attitude of upper schools, claiming that they should pay more attention to the influences of their entrance examinations on the ELT in middle schools. The situation was, incidentally, exactly the same with entrance examinations to state universities at that time (Morimura, 1937).

Nagahara, who was also very much concerned about the negative backwash of ill-balanced entrance examinations on the ELT in middle schools, made the following five recommendations in the same year (Nagahara, 1932, pp. 165-170).

(1) Introduction of paragraph reading tests

By means of paragraph reading tests, it is possible to test students' reading ability more economically and efficiently, especially their ability to grasp the gist of a paragraph. Paragraph reading tests enable teachers to save time in marking as they are relieved of the need to read students' entire translations. If the aim of ELT in Specialized Schools is to develop the ability to read original English works and grasp the gists of paragraphs quickly, then this type of testing is obviously the best technique for assessing such ability. Nagahara recommends the following four techniques as being useful:

(a) After students have read the paragraph(s), they answer in Japanese questions asked in English in order to check their understanding of what they have read.

(b) The same questions as above are asked in Japanese and students answer them in Japanese.

Answers to both (a) and (b) can be short and simple.

(c) Students work on multiple-choice questions set in Japanese.

(d) Students answer true-false questions set in Japanese.

(2) Testing vocabulary

Now that a variety of textbooks are available, the words and phrases students will master are not identical. An effort should thus be made to select a standard vocabulary.

(3) Development of standardized tests

Standardized tests for assessing every area of ability in English should be developed. They enable teachers to adjust their pace of teaching and to compare the outcomes of their teaching among students, classes, and schools. Moreover, they stimulate both teachers and students to make further efforts. Standardized tests offer highly accurate and reliable data on students' success / failure in the entrance examinations and contribute to mitigating the so-called "entrance examination evil." They function as yardsticks by which students can estimate their potential.

(4) Testing composition in English

In marking composition, two fundamentally different approaches have been identified. One is to put an emphasis on linguistic forms (grammatical correctness) and the other is to attach more importance on the efficiency of transmission of messages. It often happens, therefore, that teachers give different marks to the same answer. In order to avoid such inconsistency, it is essential to draw up criteria by which students' answers are to be judged prior to the marking. We should also refrain from asking students to use extremely difficult words in composition tests. Furthermore, a much more fundamental decision needs to be made as to whether composition tests should be imposed on students at all. If they are essential, then the level of attainment expected should be made clear to students.

(5) Reality and importance of test items

In English composition and grammar tests, we find items whose contents or meanings are totally unrealistic. Some true-false tests are utterly biased, personal opinions. We should be careful not to set such imperfect items lest they should discourage students' interest in learning English.

We have summarized above the main complaints and protests made by middle schools in the early Showa era. To our regret, some of these complaints are still being made with respect to today's entrance examinations to upper schools.

CHAPTER V

Evaluation of Communicative Competence

There is a growing awareness in the ELT profession that to serve present and very obvious future needs, more emphasis than ever before must be put on fostering aural-oral abilities. This implies that adequate testing techniques or tools for evaluating aural-oral skills need to be developed and be readily available to classroom teachers.

This final chapter attempts to review the endeavors made thus far in the quest for efficient techniques that can serve to evaluate the communicative competence of Japanese learners.

5.1 Overview

It might be a surprise to many Japanese to learn that, historically, teaching in Japanese higher education institutions was substantially carried out orally. During the first half of the Meiji era, there were few Japanese teaching staff in institutions of higher education who were sufficiently qualified to conduct tertiary education adequately. As a result, most subjects were taught in English by American and British staff. Exceptionally, medical education was provided in German. Most of the communication in the lecture rooms was, therefore, aural-oral.

The above practice was, however, exceptional in the long history of education in Japan in that it took place at a time when Japan had to modernize her education hurriedly in order to catch up with Western countries and when higher education opportunities were strictly limited to a very small number of elite students. It was, so to speak, a flower grown in a greenhouse, well taken care of by the new government.

As mentioned in Chapter II, the educational system for middle schools was formally established around the middle of the Meiji era, following which the number of middle schools increased rapidly. Cramming for the entrance examinations to upper schools soon started, and became a nation-wide practice in the Taisho era. Although, as we saw in the preceding chapter, proposals for reform were made by some leading educators, their voices were smothered by the overwhelming wave of "ELT for the sake of entrance examination." The ill-balanced entrance examinations criticized by Mtsuoka and Nagahara persisted. Under such circumstances, it was almost impossible for middle schools to pursue any fresh ELT ideal in their classrooms. In this respect, the situation in Japan was in striking contrast with that of the United States, where foreign language teachers were well aware of the significance of aural-oral skills as early as the 1930s, and continued to steadily improve on and introduce innovations into foreign language teaching.

At this point, a glance at the trend in the foreign language testing in the U. S. in the above period might be enlightening, as well as being useful in accurately tracing subsequent developments in Japan.

Keeping pace with steps toward the oral approach to language teaching, techniques for testing aural-oral skills were devised and tried in high schools. According to Lundeberg (1929, p. 196), four main techniques were available, viz. *causerie* (talk), *extempore* (extension), interpreter test, and dictation. However, the reliability of these techniques was generally low, and foreign language teachers did not regard them as functional.

Meanwhile, efforts to devise better techniques for assessing aural-oral skills were also made at the university level. As aural skills were considered easier to judge than oral ones, aural tests were introduced in the classroom first under the name of "audition tests." The following tasks were included in the tests (Lundeberg, 1929, pp. 198-201):

(1) Questions and answers in the foreign language
(2) Sentence completion by filling in blanks in the mother tongue
(3) Matching words by listening to definitions of their meaning
(4) Multiple-choice tests in pronunciation, vocabulary, phrases, sentences, and paragraphs
(5) Dictation

The techniques proposed were all really innovative, and they became the prototypes of current test items most teachers are familiar with today.

As for the assessment of oral skills, pronunciation tests were introduced in the early 1940s by Haley (1941, pp. 390-393). A Language

Achievement Scale, designed to enable language teachers to make a more global, meaningful assessment of their students' progress, also appeared slightly earlier (Sammartino, 1938, pp. 429-432). In 1944, a remarkably modern aural-oral proficiency test in the interview format was devised, which was indeed epoch-making (Kaulfers, 1944, pp. 136-150).

Harold E. Palmer's visit to Japan in the very same period might have been a rare chance to reform the grammar-translation-soaked ELT at the secondary school level. In spite of Palmer's ardent efforts, however, Japanese secondary schools were not mature enough to accept the Oral Method he advocated. In addition, the rapid progress made in the U.S. did not become known to Japanese teachers of English because Palmer went back to Britain in 1936. The militaristic, nationalistic climate in the late 1930s and the early 1940s had an adverse effect on the continuous transmission to Japan of information about reforms being made abroad. Under such circumstances, ELT as a whole declined and fell into a slumber, to say nothing of innovation in the evaluation of aural-oral skills.

After World War II, the new "Course of Study" era arrived in the postwar Japan and ELT started afresh, based on the new, modern concept of language teaching and learning. After an extensive survey of tests used in Japanese secondary classrooms around the mid 1960s, Inamura made the following comments on the general nature of the aural-oral tests he had surveyed (Inamura, 1970, iv):

> Most items assess students' memory of language elements only; there are very few that assess functional skills directly. In research into testing, it is hoped that emphasis will be placed on the development of techniques which will assess the latter skills adequately. What teachers must do now is to try to design functional, skill-based tests and to replace the

current knowledge-based tests with the new ones.

Tests such as Inamura envisaged did not, however, appear immediately. Judging from the standards of research in testing at that time, it would have been almost impossible to design new tests that would satisfy Inamura's conditions.

The development of aural-oral tests also suffered from a shift in attention in ELT circles toward the issue of the nature of language learning. The controversy between Audio-Lingual Habit Theory and Cognitive Code-Learning Theory, which lasted nearly ten years, made it virtually impossible for teachers to embark on designing pilot tests of the kind that were needed in language classrooms.

After ten years' turmoil, however, the controversy began to subside around the middle of the 1970s, and real endeavors to design aural-oral test, or "communicative tests" as they were commonly called in the seventies, were made by pioneering teachers. In their attempts, Backman's model shown in Chapter II was an essential guide in delineating the construct of language competence, from which the new idea of communicative tests could be derived. In fact it can safely be said that most of the communicative tests developed thereafter were more than a little based on his model.

Today, interviews, pair work, and group work are exploited for direct testing of communicative competence. For written tests, authentic materials, e.g. newspaper or magazine articles, explanatory notes, timetables, and sightseeing pamphlets are being used extensively.

5.2 Future Outlook

In this section we will discuss further the issue of "direct testing" refered to above, since this is really the very key to the success of communicative testing.

5.2.1 Types of Tasks

In communicative testing, students are required to work on a certain number of tasks given to them. In designing a communicative test, the first thing for the designer to do is to choose the types of tasks which will reflect the students' actual communication situations in their everyday lives. Unfortunately, there are no guidelines offered by Japanese educators and researchers on the selection of appropriate communicative tasks. Indeed, we have to look to research findings from overseas.

There is a consensus among researchers that two types of tasks should be imposed for beginners: *transactional* tasks (activities to get services or exchange things) and *interpersonal* tasks (activities for maintaining personal relationships). It is argued that by setting tasks of these two types, a balanced coverage of language functions is maintained, thus freeing students form the possibility of biased assessment (Brown and Yule, 1983, pp. 11-16; Nunan, 1989, pp. 113-115; Nunan, 1991, p.6). By imposing transactional tasks, we can test a number of essential functions, such as reporting, asking, requesting, etc., while interpersonal task will test functions like greeting, introducing oneself / others, attracting attention, etc..

In this connection, a survey of the functions which appear in current English textbooks for Japanese junior and senior high school students should also be made, as this is a prerequisite for fair evaluation. It is unfair and discouraging to include functions students might not have encountered in their lessons. A glance at several of the main English textbooks for junior high schools reveals that students will actually encounter a considerable number of functions during their three years of schooling. A similar survey should also be done on textbooks for senior high schools in order to obtain general information about the coverage and distribution of the functions available to the communicative test designer.

5.2.2 Degree of Task Difficulty

Tasks in communicative tests should match students' proficiency levels. Tasks that are too demanding might discourage students from communicating in the foreign language, while those that are much too easy can bore students and fail to give them the incentive to communicate. Five factors which condition the difficulty of tasks have been cited by Nunan (1991, pp. 24-28; pp. 47-49):

(1) Vocabulary
(2) Sentence structure
(3) Topic
(4) Number of items and persons
(5) Type of relationship

A brief explanation of the last factor might be needed. A relationship can be classified into three categories; static, dynamic, or abstract. A static relationship is represented by, for example, "describing diagrams or patterns." Among dynamic relationships are included "describing a car crash," "recounting how a piece of equipment works," and "retelling a narrative based on a cartoon strip." Abstract relationships include "expressing one's opinion concerning a specific topic," and "justifying a certain action."

When we actually come to design a communicative task, it is advisable to have a table or matrix with the above factors in it. Using this table for reference, we can then adjust the level of difficulty of the task we are designing. By so doing, it is also possible for the designer to set fair and representative tasks.

5.2.3 Evaluation Techniques

Techniques that have so far been exploited for evaluation can be grouped into two categories:

(1) The examiner evaluates the student's performance based on grade / level descriptions made beforehand.

(2) The student works on the graded tasks. Tasks successfully completed automatically represent the grade to be assigned.

The drawback of technique (1) is that the grade given tends to be subjective, and accordingly unreliable. Technique (2) has a similar drawback in that the grading of tasks is apt to be subjective and arbitrary. Developing reliable techniques is an absolutely essential requisite for the promotion and improvement of communicative testing.

5.2.4 Elimination of Examiner's Influence on Oral Interview

An oral interview is a common technique used in communicative testing. In the interview, the examiner should endeavor to be as neutral as possible in order to obtain the reliable data from the student. Since inconsistency or instability on the part of examiner is fatal to successful testing, proper measures should be taken during and after the interview. In this regard, the following guidelines have so far been accumulated (Weir, 1993, pp. 26-27):

(1) Elimination of examiner's influence during interview
   (a) Thorough understanding of the testing procedures
   (b) Establishment of *rapport* between examiner and examinee
   (c) Check of the clarity of questions and directions
   (d) Provision of sufficient prompts and encouragement of the unsuccessful interviewee
   (e) Training of the examiner's skills in question and answer interaction

(2) Consistency in processing data after interview
   (a) Thorough understanding of the assessment criteria
   (b) Trial marking / grading
   (c) Review of the procedures
   (d) Follow-up checks

5.2.5 Repair of Breakdown in Oral Interview

In a written test, even when students can not answer the questions, the execution of the test itself seldom comes to a standstill. In an oral interview, however, a student's failure to respond often baffles both examiners (teachers) and students themselves, and the entire execution of testing can collapse halfway. In order to use the oral interview technique extensively in communicative tests, the causes of breakdowns and means of overcoming them must be investigated.

We know from experience that breakdown will

often occur under the following circumstances:

(1) When directions or cues are not clear or sufficient, students often fail to respond. For beginners, it might be helpful to use the mother tongue when they have difficulties in understanding what is required of them.
(2) There is a tendency to impose heavier tasks in oral interviews. To avoid this, we should understand students' ability accurately before embarking on an oral interview test.
(3) When a sufficient time for reply is not given during the interview, a student's performance tends to be imperfect due to the pressure to communication. Experienced examiners know this well, and adjust the lengths of the pause during the interview accordingly. Novice examiners, however, are likely to use shorter pauses. When yes-no or simple word responses are expected as answers, short pauses might work better,

but for heavier, demanding tasks, such as "describing reasons / causes," "expressing opinions," and "criticizing others," longer pauses should be provided.

When a breakdown does occur during an oral interview, the techniques shown below are normally utilized to repair and maintain the interaction:

(1) The examiner repeats the question the way it was asked initially. No definite guideline is available as the number of times it should be repeated, which will be determined by the student's ability and the difficulty of the task.
(2) The examiner presents a "comparable" task(s) prepared beforehand. The number of tasks given again varies in accordance with the student's ability and the degree of difficulty.

In this final chapter, a historical review, though brief, of communicative testing in Japan has been attempted. Through this review, it has become apparent that we owe a great deal to research findings from abroad, and that we need to make further efforts for ourselves to ensure these findings are made more applicable to the Japanese foreign language classroom.

REFERENCES

Ando, Shoichi, et al. eds. (1991) *A Dictionary of Key Terms in English Language Education,* Osaka: Zoshindo.

Aoki, Shoroku, et al. (1989) *Eigo no tesutingu: jissenteki apurochi* (Testing in English: A Practical Approach), Tokyo: Kairyudo.

Bachman, Lyle F. (1990) *Fundamental Consideration in Language Testing,* Oxford: Oxford University Press.

Brown, Gillian and G. Yule (1983) *Teaching the Spoken Language,* Cambridge: Cambridge University Press.

Coleman, Algernon (1929)*The Teaching of Modern Foreign Languages in the United States* (Publication of the American and Canadian Committees on Modern Languages) 12, New York: The Macmillan Company.

Haley, S.M.P. (1941) Evaluation in Oral French, *The Modern Language Journal,* 25 (5), 390-393.

Hashimoto, Juji, et al. (1979) *Kyoikuhyoka yosetsu* (An Outline of Educational Evaluation), Tokyo: Tosho Bunka.

Hatori, Hiroyoshi (1962) Eigogakuryoku no kozo (The Nature of English Proficiency), *Kyoikugijyutsu:*

gakushushinri (Teaching Techniques: Educational Psychology), 4 (12), 94-98.

Inamura, Matsuo (1970) *Hyoka to sokutei* (Measurement and Evaluation), Tokyo: Kenkyusha.

Institute for Research in Language Teaching, ed. (1943) *Gaikokugo kyojyuho* (Methods of Teaching Foreign Languages), Tokyo: Kaitakusha.

Ishikawa, Rinshiro (1911) Shikenmondai ni tsuite (On Question Items of Examinations), *Eigo kyoju* (Teaching English), 4 (4), 19-28. Tokyo: Meicho Fukyu Kai, 1985.

Kaneko, Kenji (1923) *Kotoba no kenkyu to kotoba no shido* (The Study of Languages and Teaching), Tokyo: Hobunkan.

Kaulfers, Walter V. (1944) Wartime Development in Modern Language Achievement Testing, *The Modern Language Journal*, 28 (2), 136-150.

Kimura, Shigeharu (1917) Requirements for the Entrance Examination for Schools of Higher Grade, *Eigo kyoju* (Teaching English), 10 (1), 1-7. Tokyo: Meicho Fukyu Kai, 1985.

Kyokasho Kenkyu Sentaa (Center for Research on School Textbooks) ed. (1984) *Kyusei chutogakko kyokanaiyo no hensen* (Changes in the Contents of School Subjects for Middle Schools under the Middle School Order), Tokyo: Gyosei.

Lado, Robert (1961) *Language Testing: The Construction*

and Use of Foreign Language Tests, London: Longman.

Lundeberg, Olav K. (1929) Recent Development in Audition Speech Tests, *The Modern Language Journal*, 14 (3), 193-202.

Matsuoka, Totaro (1932) Eigo kyoju to nyugakushiken mondai (Teaching English and Entrance Examinations), *Eigo eibungaku ronso* (The Journal of English Language and Literature), 1 (2), 134-147. Tokyo: Meicho Fukyu Kai, 1986.

Ministry of Education (1951) *The Suggested Course of Study in English for Lower and Upper Secondary Schools (Tentative Plan)*, Tokyo: Chuo Tosho.

Ministry of Education, Science and Culture (1980) *Japan's Modern Educational System: A History of the First Hundred Years*, Tokyo: Printing Bureau, Ministry of Finance.

Morimura, Yutaka (1937) *Zenkoku kanritsudaigaku nyushi eigomondai seikai* (Keys to the State University Entrance Examinations: English), Tokyo: Kenkyusha

Nagahara, Toshio (1932) Gakuryoku kenteiho ni kansuru shomondai to sono kosatsu (A Review of the Issues on Language Testing), *Eigo eibungaku ronso* (The Journal of English Language and Literature), 1 (2), 148-172. Tokyo: Meicho Fukyu Kai, 1986.

Nagahara, Toshio (1936) *Shiken to gakushu* (Examinations and Learning), Tokyo: Kenkyusha.

Nunan, David (1989) *Designing Tasks for the Communicative Classrooms*, Cambridge: Cambridge University Press.

Nunan, David (1991) *Language Teaching Methodology*, New York: Prentice Hall.

Okakura, Yoshisaburo (1911) *Eigo kyoiku* (Teaching English), Tokyo: Hakubunkan.

Okuda, Shinjyo ed. (1985) *Kyokakyoiku hyakunenshi* (A History of the First Hundred Years of School Subject Education), Tokyo: Kenpakusha.

Omura, Kiyoshi, K. Takanashi, and S. Deki eds. (1980) *Eigokyoikushi shiryo* (Research Data on the History of English Language Education) 1, Tokyo: Tokyo Horei Shuppan.

Palmer, Harold E. (1927) The New-Type Examinations, *The Bulletin of the Institute for Research in English Teaching*, 34, Appendix, 29Pp. Rpt. as *The Bulletin of IRET: Supplements and Notes*, 7. Tokyo: Meicho Fukyu Kai, 1985.

Palmer, Harold E. (1933) A New-Type Examination, *The Bulletin of the Institute for Research in English Teaching*, 92, 5-6. Rpt. as *The Bulletin of IRET*, Vol. 2. Tokyo: Meicho Fukyu Kai, 1985.

Research Group on Postwar Educational Reform Materials, National Institute for Educational Research, ed. (1980) *Monbusho gakushushidoyoryo: gaikokugo hen* (Ministry of Education's Courses of Study for Foreign

Languages) 19, Tokyo: Nihon Tosho Sentaa.

Sammartino, Peter (1938) A Language Achievement Scale, *The Modern Language Journal*, 22 (6), 429-432.

Sasaki, Miyuki (2008) The 150-year history of English language assessment in Japanese education, *Language Testing*, 25 (1), 63-83.

Savignon, Sandra (1983) *Communicative Competence: Theory and Classroom Practice*, Reading, Mass.: Addison-Wesley.

Shikata, Jitsukazu (1971) *Gakkokyoiku ni okeru sokutei to hyoka* (Measurement and Evaluation in School Education), Tokyo: Meiji Tosho.

Spolsky, Bernard (1994) The beginning of language testing as a profession, In James E. Alatis, ed. *Georgetown University Round Table on Language and Linguistics 1994: Educational Linguistics, Crosscultural Communication, and Global Interdependence*, Washington, D. C.: Georgetown University Press, 88-101.

Takahashi, Hikosaburo (1931) Shin-yomoku ni yoru eigoka toriatsukai jissai-an (A Plan for the New ELT Based on the Revised 1931 Syllabuses), *Eigo eibungaku ronso* (The Journal of English Language and Literature), 1 (1), 12-19. Tokyo: Meicho Fukyu Kai, 1986.

Takehara, Tsuneta (1936) *Chutogakko eigokyozai no kagakuteki hensanho* (A Scientific Approach to the

Compilation of ELT Materials for Middle Schools), Tokyo: Taishukan.

Takenaka, Jiro (1938) Nyutaipu tesuto no jissai (The New-Type Tests: Classroom Practice), *Eigo no kenkyu to kyoju* (The Study and Teaching of English), 7 (2), 42-44.; 7 (3), 75-76.; 7 (4), 106-107.; 7 (5), 152-153. Tokyo: Hon no Tomo Sha, 1994.

Tanaka, Masamichi (1987) Kyoshitsu no dentatsu tesuto (Communicative Tests for the Classroom), *The Research Bulletin of Chugoku Academic Society for English Language Education*, 17, 209-218.

Tanaka, Masamichi (1993) Komyunikeshion-shiko ni do taiosuruka (Approaches and Methods in Communicative Language Teaching), *Eigo kyoiku* (The English Teachers' Magazine), 42 (1), 14-18.

Tanaka, Masamichi (1994) Komyunikeshion-noryoku to tesuto (Testing and Communicative Competence), *Eigo kyoiku* (The English Teachers' Magazine), 43 (4), 26-28.

The United States Education Mission to Japan (1946) *Report of the United States Education Mission to Japan: Submitted to the Supreme Commander for the Allied Powers*, Tokyo, March 30, [69 Pp.]

Tsuchiya, Sumio (1973) Eigo kyoju-gakushu no hyoka ni okeru tesuto no riyo (Using Tests in the Teaching and Learning of English), In Shigeo Ouchi ed. *Kenkyu to hyoka* (Research and Evaluation) 5, Tokyo: Kenkyusha, 29-85.

Valdman, Albert (1978) Communicative Use of Language and Syllabus Design, *Foreign Language Annals*, 11 (5), 567-578.

Watari, Toshio (1938) Eigo toan o seisashite (An Analysis of Candidates' Answers to the Entrance Examination), In English Department, Yokohama Specialized School ed. *Eigo kai zasshi* (The Journal of English Society), 49-51.

Weir, Cyril (1993) *Understanding and Developing Language Tests*, New York: Prentice Hall.

Wilkins, David (1978) *Notional Syllabuses*, Oxford: Oxford University Press.

INDEX

A
American and Canadian Committees on Modern Languages 37
Ando, Shoichi 52
Assistant Language Teacher 21-22
Audio-Lingual Habit Theory 108
aural-oral skills 37, 46, 104
Authorized English Textbooks 61

B
Bachman, Lyle F. 59

C
causerie 104
Chugakkorei (The Middle School Order) 24
Chutogakko Eigokyozai no Kagakuteki Hensanho (A Scientific Approach to the Compilation of ELT Materials for Secondary Schools) 15
Cognitive Code-Learning Theory 108
Coleman, Algernon 37
communicative competence 58, 101
Communicative Language Teaching 5, 20
communicative test 21,108
completion test 16
Completion Type 14
correlation 8

D
Dewey, John 9
Dictation 25, 27, 29, 36, 40, 104
discourse competence 59

E
Eigo Kyoiku (Teaching English) 12
English as "speech" 46,47, 48,49,51
entrance examination 83,84, 103
evaluation 11

extempore 104

G

Gaikokugo Kyojyuho (Methods of Teaching Foreign Languages) 16

Gakusei (The Education System Order) 3

Gestalt psychology 10

Gogaku Kyoiku Kenkyusho (The Institute for Research in Language Teaching) 16

grammatical competence 59

H

Hani, Motoko 73

Hatori, Hiroyoshi 52

Hellen Keller 73

higher elementary school (Koto Shogakko) 30

Hiroshima Higher Normal School 36-37, 39

Hornby, A. S. 17

I

illocutionary competence 59

Inamura, Matsuo 107, 108

informal test 16

intelligence test 8

interpersonal task 110

Ishikawa, Rinshiro 84

J

JET Program 22

Jishu Eibunten (English Grammar Self-Taught) 72

Jiyu Gakuen 73

K

Kanda, Naibu 62

Kaneko, Kenji 13

Katayama, Hiroshi 66

Kimura, Shigeharu 87

Kotoba no Kenkyu to Kotoba no Shido (The Study of Languages and Teaching) 13

Kumamoto, Kenjiro 64

Kyoikurei (The Education Order) 25

L

Lado, Robert 54

M

Matsuoka, Totaro 95

measurement movement 8

multiple choice test 16

N

Nagahara, Toshio 14, 36, 96

New-Type Examinations, The 14

Nunan, David 111, 112

O

objective test 8, 19

Okakura, Yoshisaburo 12

Ono, Keijiro 71

oral interview 114
organizational competence 59
Osaka Prefectural Toyonaka Middle School 95

P

Palmer, Harold Edward 14, 15, 32, 73, 106
parse 62, 65, 67, 69
Penmanship 27, 29, 36
pragmatic competence 59

Q

quiz 61

R

rapport 115
reliability 8, 19
repair 116
Report of the United States Education Mission to Japan 41-42, 43

S

Savignon, Sandra 58
Selection, or Recognition Type 14
Shiken to Gakushu (Examinations and Learning) 15
silent reading test 16
standard test 16
standardized test 8, 98

sociolinguistic competence 59
strategic competence 59
structural linguistics 54
Suggested Course of Study in English for Lower and Upper Secondary Schools (Tentative Plan),The 18

T

Takehara, Tsuneta 15
Takahashi, Hikosaburo 39
textual competence 59
Tokyo Higher Normal School 84
transactional task 110
True-False Type 14
Tsuchiya, Sumio 54

V

validity 8, 19

W

Watari, Toshio 91
Wilkins, David 21

Y

Yamaguchi Higher Commercial School 87, 91-92
Yamazaki, S. 71
Yokohama Specialized School 91